Big Sexy Lunch

Roxy Dunn

VERVE
POETRY PRESS

BIRMINGHAM

PUBLISHED BY VERVE POETRY PRESS
https://vervepoetrypress.com
mail@vervepoetrypress.com

FIRST PUBLISHED MAR 2020

Printed and bound in the UK
by Positive Print, Birmingham

ISBN: 978-1-912565-37-5

CONTENTS

Acknowledgements

For Jono

Big Sexy Lunch

Big Sexy Lunch

I advise a big sexy lunch
The six course Italian kind
Beginning with champagne
Warm smoked eel
Pickled blackberries
On a bed of beetroot
A big sexy lunch
Moving onto tortelli
With lobster and tarragon
Transcending hunger
So three courses in to
The sea bass ragu
You begin to feed
Entirely out of greed
Making the act of eating
A new realm of experience
As the Mount Etna wine
Is nearing depletion
It assists you in articulating
Seemingly complicated
Philosophical ideas
With such concision
You congratulate your conversation
On both its content and delivery
Unashamedly concluding
That a big sexy lunch
Is not solely for pleasure

But the development of humanity
And the growth of our species
A big sexy lunch
With Sardinian cheese
Amalfi lemon tart
Double espresso which
Despite the caffeine
Can't pull you out of
Your hazy satisfaction
So back at your home
For the rest of the afternoon
You lie on the bed
Venetian blinds closed
Not summoning the energy
For actual sex
You touch each other
With your nearest hands
Producing yet more
Groaning sensations
And you feel that death
Although unappealing
Would not in this instant
Be as intolerable a proposition
As it were before
The big sexy lunch
For the simple reason
Whilst you haven't achieved
All the things you intended
You are in this moment
Undeniably living
Your best life

Relationship Advice

You'll accidentally leave
the string on the flowers he gave you
so it looks like a noose floating
in a vase; try not to read in to this
avoid symbolism in general

When you dream of sharing
his one set of arms and legs
you'll start to think your love's
unique; don't get excited
imagining his epitaph

Money or war will help
not too much but a lot
kiss him as if it's your last
as if a bomb is about to fall
no one can say: *you didn't try*

August Conker

You're at a party with Damon Albarn
I'm printing a 5x7 photo of a conker
I feel like a spinster at twenty-eight

What's the alternative? A two bed semi
on a new build estate in Didcot discussing
sandwich fillings and trips to the sea

I dread Saturdays in summer like a sickness
in Finsbury Park even the shiny teens
are rolling around in couplets on the grass

I think my default setting is nostalgia
I've been reading Frank O'Hara on the train
back from Cheltenham, I've become too self-aware

I'm not blaming Frank for my hot blues
I'm actually grateful for his encouragement
even if it means I'll be true and lonely

for another sixty years, even
if this sun is making everyone and everything
so horribly beautiful and appealing

There's an Urgency!

Unbuttoning
the tops of our jeans
pulling off our own shirts
chests skin-on-skin

Lips tingling
with vinegar residues
exchanging pulp
between stinging mouths

Suede plays on Spotify
shards spike the duvet
we're like a ridge cut crisp ad
selling *intimacy*

List

Because you haven't text
I've compiled a list of your problems
to ween myself off you:

1.   *I think you might be provincial*
        you try too hard to be cultivated
        which makes me suspicious

2.   *You could be more succinct in speech*
        what you think sounds intelligent
        is actually verbose

3.   *Inconsequential things annoy you*
        like bad latte-art and wine
        with a screw-cap

4.   *You are relatively small*

5.   *You cum relatively quickly*

6.   *You have pretty hair but lack balls*

7.   *You've now just text but the list now exists*
        which is currently the new problem

Sweet Casanova

(After Ruby Andrews)

I scour *The Guardian* on my way to the club
to buff up on Aleppo before we grind

The t-shirt in front says *No Regrets*
promo for the Dreams Sale poster above

Does working for an NGO make you good in part?
You're as incongruous as Trump figure-skating

I've tried not waxing, sticking north of the river
blocking you on WhatsApp, you said I was smart

At Elephant and Castle I muse on polygamy
it smells aqua-green, tastes conceptually appealing

According to Emily Witt's, *Future Sex*
if life was Burning Man we'd dare to live freely

The strobes on this floor make your face flick
out of focus, a metaphor for your fleetingness

Alpha men pushing prams along Church Street
prove it's possible to have sex-appeal and not be a dick

Perhaps a baby could give me closure
stop me watching sharks at 4am on YouTube

You're hallowed in the light with the last track of the night
Sweet Casanova (your playing days aren't over)

Hedda

Despite your strategies
and Mensa IQ
not even you
comprehend your objective

Let's get Drake on the Sonos
swig Malbec semi-clothed
you'll have a wife
before Labour get elected

I'll find out from LinkedIn
she shoots herself (lol)
enigma gets tiring*

*even in Stockwell

July 24th

Eighty-six years ago today
the Serpentine opened to women
to swim without fear of arrest

I'm lost on the Heath searching
for these ponds, it's thirty-degrees
in Hampstead, what's with all the beards?

Two girls in front are talking
about their exes, how they're okay
now they're with *new men*

Don't tell me fullness is found
from a man, I'll shoot myself
or dehydrate, a more feasible option

There's a lot of holding of hands
and leads, my palms are empty
if my mother were here she'd say

Find a good book, easy
for her with a husband and a spaniel
Now I'm in the water I relish

the freedom, no one knows I'm here
I could just bob under (not
to get all Virginia Woolf about it)

At lunchtime today we spoke
on the phone, big literary things
are happening for you, how apt

I was sat in Bloomsbury Square
Remember Southease, cider
along the Ouse, Monk House

all our Sussex hours? If love
was just lunchtimes of erudite chat
we would have worked completely

But I have this need to swim
with ducks and reeds, you said
it was *sweet*. It was wild

Exes at Lunch

It ought to be encouraging:
proof of love's stability

but the past becomes disturbed
the kinder feelings persist

pulling laughter and light until
the old disappointments are forgot

The frayed tether's return is unexplained
why in this safe embrace our arms serve

up everything lost, and not gained

Hyde Park

Today Hyde Park is hotter
than Hawaii, Buckingham Palace
is the backdrop of the sky
you've got to buy in to it, believe

I can do this. Take a selfie, smile
rent a Boris Bike, ride
like it's the end of summer, not
February the twenty-third

Get enchanted by palaces and fountains
trust heat and light can be made
into feeling, let all of this
convince you, *I am in love with Daniel*

Weeds

Kanye is supposedly the Bob Dylan of our age
something tells me we've been short-changed

Yoga's got more qualified instructors than participants
turning hobbies into work is considered an accomplishment

Kat in Luxembourg asked *what is your joy?*
as if I already knew it and my boredom was a ploy

The pub feels repetitive, Netflix makes me bitter
I can't get addicted to Trump's Twitter

Listening to Drake what would I rather?
That's the point of R&B, it makes you work harder

I'll double my circuit, play *Light Up* on a loop
lap the sleeveless boys in Finsbury Park shooting hoops

It alarms me when people say my characters aren't likeable
they're based primarily on versions of me

When I smiled at that woman in the queue out of loneliness
it made me feel ashamed like being bloated on the pull

I need someone next to me to make me watch TV
or else I frequently forget to look at the screen

Last night I had to Google *how to Giff*
I'm letting down Gen Y, I'm meant to know technology

I can't retain facts or imperial measurements
I've stopped eating meat I'm not even sure why

If I squint under the bridge at Harringay Green Lanes
the sun and saxophonist could kid me into confidence

The sweet red peppers on the corner of Dostlar
are tightly stacked like rows of shining buttocks

The weeds in the garden must absolutely stay
they are so yellow and sure of who they are

Robinsons

This weak lemon barley
tastes of our childhood

Trampolining in our underwear
on school summer nights

B*Witched on cassette
singing *C'est La Vie*

Bouncing to be beautiful
American and sixteen

I wonder if you're satisfied
or married at least

Black-Eyed Bear

You are riddled
with shit sex
one-way chat
still I come

back, I want
to wake in
your gruff
hairy lock
drink sweet
strong tea
from your unmade
lair, teach

your swaggering
grace how roughly
to love

Equation

(After Nisha Ramayya)

happiness is growth
trust Socrates on this
affirm an empty swimming pool
happiness is unannounced
study philosophers
assume the perpendicular
happiness is rogue
cultivate not knowing
wine and drugs are welcome
happiness is inconclusive
adjust your mind
there isn't really a limit
happiness is celebratory
yes college was a gift
hold onto blue and yellow
happiness is bold
let go of interesting
self-awareness is a rarity
happiness is an art
write to feel most like yourself
deny Hollywood your poem

regardless of pain
dismiss self-help books
put your faith in Derren Brown
regardless of impatience
over-question the point
borrow lines from Neil Hannon
regardless of copyright
embrace self-doubt
it's not a finished equation
regardless of neatness
find an angle that suits
visualise a gymnast
regardless of losing
still appreciate in hindsight
keep kindness in the foreground
regardless of nerves
be that old winner – nice
work to feel less like others
regardless of imperfection
own the rights to you
resist the urge to cash in

Falling

Golden boy
it's not your curled
curtains and springy
step or that you
make me say

yes

four times
every morning
as you go down
beneath the sheet
it is none of that

per se

Grey Area

Between beauty and cruelty
are examples of grey area:

Fabritius' *Goldfinch*
Han Qiaoni's bound feet

the draped fox stole
around the singer's neck

declaring you love me
at my final boarding call

Glosa on Frank O'Hara's *Mayakovsky*

'Now I am quietly waiting for
the catastrophe of my personality
to seem beautiful again,
and interesting, and modern.' – *Mayakovsky,* Frank O'Hara

I thought whiskey would make it cooler
the reality of working for a living
all that idolising owning a study
culminates in this: a generic green lamp
and my un-needed manuscript
I still naively hope there is more
to me than the quality of these pages
even though Hopper is reliably honest
there is always someone's bullshit at the door
Now I am quietly waiting for

a day without getting dressed
and eating everything from a microwave
did you know you can cook egg in a mug?
I took a trip to the country and I slept
like a metaphorical log. The pheasant
made me grimace but the air was breezy
I insisted on singing under the stars
and shed a tear; moved by my own voice
as indulgent and narcissistic as frankly
the catastrophe of my personality

I don't desire to shoot a deer
or get blood on my hands
but it was good to feel clay
my lack of unresolved
issues has become the issue
it's necessary to regress in rain
to stomp and imagine
the puddles as grief
am I mad to want pain
to seem beautiful again?

Back in the city taking a shower
feels progressive, I used up
all the hot water in my country bath
it was selfish but I wanted the burn
What's meant by our other selves?
There are things I ought to learn
like driving a car and stoicism;
my grandmother's watch is a daily
reminder: I want life to feel earned
and interesting, and modern.

Desert Island Discs

Asimo's Run (Paper Tiger)
Cecilia (Simon & Garfunkel)
Sexuality (Billy Bragg)
Hotline Bling (Drake)
I Like (The Divine Comedy)
Finishing the Hat (Stephen Sondheim)
Strangers in the Night (Frank Sinatra)
The Lark Ascending (Vaughan Williams)

Luxury item: pen & paper
Book: Staying Alive (Bloodaxe)

You once purchased Electronic Space-Funk
Remember heartache can be fun
Fuck more/worry less
You're still a feminist
There is joy in sexiness
You're not like other women
Nostalgic for pre-Tinder
A token classical

You're more generic than you think
You're going to survive this

AMS – LCY

We departed at 21.15
Ed Sheeran played on the headphones
of the balding man next to us

I attempted to read Anne Tyler
your paprika hand gripped
my left and maybe lingered

We landed at 21.15
I couldn't work out what
if anything, had not happened

Rudie's

Part of love is letting go of leanness
eating late-night dumplings at Rudie's
dough settling on our softening stomachs

Spooning we cup the roundness and dips
of our sides and arses like hot smooth dunes
overlapping each other rolling in expanse

Light comes early through the blind
the day stretches out pink and vast
I cannot sleep from fullness

ACKNOWLEDGEMENTS

'Grey Area' first appeared in issue 171 of *Orbis*.

Thank you to Stuart Bartholomew and Verve Poetry Press, thanks also to Ali Lewis, Kathryn Maris, and the other staff and students at the Poetry School who helped critique a number of poems in this pamphlet.

ABOUT THE AUTHOR

Roxy Dunn's debut pamphlet *Clowning,* published by Eyewear in 2016, is their highest selling pamphlet to date and was described by PN Review as 'quick-fire, appealing, lit by humorous warmth.' Her poetry has appeared in *The Rialto, Orbis* and *Ofi Press*, and a selection of her poems are also printed in the anthology *Podium Poets #2,* published by Nasty Little Press. She lives in North London and works as an actor and writer.

ABOUT VERVE POETRY PRESS

Verve Poetry Press is a fairly new and already award-winning press focussing hard on meeting a need in Birmingham - a need for the vibrant poetry scene here in Brum to find a way to present itself to the poetry world via publication. Co-founded by Stuart Bartholomew and Amerah Saleh, it is publishing poets from all corners of the city - poets that represent the city's varied and energetic qualities and will communicate its many poetic stories.

Added to this is a colourful pamphlet series featuring poets who have previously performed at our sister festival - and a poetry show series which captures the magic of longer poetry performance pieces by poets such as Polarbear and Matt Abbott.

Like the festival, we will strive to think about poetry in inclusive ways and embrace the multiplicity of approaches towards this glorious art.

In 2019 the press was voted Most Innovative Publisher at the Saboteur Awards, and won the Publisher's Award for Poetry Pamphlets at the Michael Marks Awards.

www.vervepoetrypress.com
@VervePoetryPres
mail@vervepoetrypress.com